Easy
To
Invest

Easy

To

Invest

Easy to Understand Mutual Fund and Investment Thumb Rule, Achieve your financial goals.

Subhajit Ghara

Cover design by [Subhajit Ghara]

ISBN: 9798897240951

Publisher: Notionpress

This book is dedicated to my parents
Ranjan Ghara
and
Purnima Bera Ghara

I am grateful to God for blessing me with such
a loving and caring family.

About The Author

Subhajit Ghara, holds a **Bachelor of Science (BSc)** degree and a **Post Graduate Diploma in Banking Service (PGDBS)**, bringing over **six years of hands-on experience in investing and financial management**. Passionate about simplifying complex financial concepts, he has dedicated their career to helping individuals make smarter money decisions.

In this book, they break down the essentials of **building financial strength** in **easy-to-understand language**, empowering readers to **invest wisely, grow wealth, and achieve financial freedom**—without the jargon.

Preface

Investing in mutual funds can be an effective way to build wealth over time, offering a diversified portfolio managed by professionals. Whether you're new to investing or looking to refine your strategy, this book is designed to guide you through the essentials of mutual fund investing. We'll explore the different types of funds, key factors to consider when selecting them, and strategies to maximize returns while managing risks. By understanding the fundamentals of mutual fund investments, you can make informed decisions to help secure your financial future. Let's begin your journey to becoming a confident investor in mutual funds.

Kolkata
January, 2025   Subhajit Ghara

Acknowledgements

I would like to express my deepest gratitude to all those who contributed to the creation of this book. First and foremost, to my family, whose unwavering support and encouragement allowed me the time and space to write. Their belief in me has been a constant source of motivation.

A special thank you to my mentors and financial experts who generously shared their knowledge, insights, and experience. Without their guidance, much of the content in this book would not have been possible. Your expertise has shaped this work in ways words can hardly capture.

Lastly, to my readers: thank you for trusting this book as a resource in your journey to financial growth and security. May it help you navigate the world of mutual fund investing with confidence and clarity.

With sincere appreciation,
Subhajit Ghara

Contents

Chapter 1

Mutual funds can be one of the best investment options in India, especially for long-term goals like retirement, children's education, or wealth creation. They offer the potential for higher returns, professional management, and diversification. However, success in mutual fund investment depends on choosing the right fund, staying invested for the long term, and aligning the investment with your financial goals and risk tolerance.

Why Mutual Funds are a Good Investment Option in India?

Strong Economic Growth:

India is one of the fastest-growing economies in the world. Factors like a young workforce, rising middle class, and increasing urbanization support robust economic growth.

The Indian stock market reflects this growth, making equity-oriented mutual funds for wealth creation over the long term.

Diversification:

Indian mutual funds offer a variety of schemes, allowing diversification across sectors, asset classes, and market capitalizations. This minimizes the risk associated with market volatility.

Regulatory Oversight:

Mutual funds in India are regulated by **SEBI (Securities and Exchange Board of India)**, ensuring transparency, investor protection, and proper fund management.

Accessibility and Affordability:

Investors can start with small amount and build their portfolios over time.

Mutual funds are accessible even to small investors, with SIPs (Systematic Investment Plans) starting as low as ₹500 per month.

Tax Benefits:

Equity Linked Savings Schemes (ELSS) provide tax deductions of up to ₹1.5 lakh under Section 80C of the Income Tax Act, so you can save your tax in your capital gain.

Professional Management:

Mutual funds are managed by professionals with expertise in analysing market trends and managing investments, ideal for investors. With out market knowledge investor's money is invest in strong and future growth companies.

Comparison with Other Investment Options in India

Investment Option	Returns	Risk	Liquidity	Tax Efficiency	Suitable For
Mutual Funds	Moderate to High	Moderate to High	High	ELSS offers tax benefits	Long-term growth, diversification

Fixed Deposits (FDs)	Low to Moderate	Low	Moderate	Interest taxable	Conservative investors
Real Estate	High (Long Term)	High	Low	Tax benefits on loans	Large capital, long-term investors
Stocks	High	High	High	Taxable on gains	High-risk appetite
Gold	Moderate	Moderate	High	Taxable on gains	Hedge against inflation

In given chart we see that, according to Indian inflation rate (more equal to 6.5%) mutual fund is the best investment option. Because there have moderate to high earning returns, high liquidity, diversification, professional management, safety and security and also tax savings option.

Before invest in mutual fund, for choose best mutual fund for myself or capital growth or future plan, please go throw this book on further next chapter all important points are discusses. So, you can easily choice best mutual fund.

***

Chapter 2

Types of Mutual Funds

Mutual funds can be broadly classified based on their structure, investment objective, and asset allocation.

Based on Structure:

- ***Open-Ended Funds:***
  Can be bought or redeemed at any time. No fixed maturity period. High liquidity.
- ***Close-Ended Funds:***
  Can only be traded on stock exchanges after the New Fund Offer (NFO) period. Have a fixed maturity period.
- ***Interval Funds:***
  A hybrid of open- and close-ended funds. Can only be bought or redeemed at specific intervals.

Based on Investment Objectives:

- ***Equity Funds:***
  Invest primarily in stocks (equities). Higher returns but also higher risk.

There are many types of funds e.g., Large-Cap fund, Mid-Cap fund, Small Cap fund, Multicap fund, Sectoral/Thematic Funds.

- *Debt Funds:*
  Invest in fixed-income securities like bonds, debentures, and money market instruments. Lower risk but moderate returns. There are many types of funds e.g., Liquid funds, Short-Term funds, Long-Term funds, Gilt funds.

- *Hybrid Funds:*
  Combine equity and debt investments. This type of funds balances the risk and returns. There are three types of funds e.g., Aggressive Hybrid Funds (higher equity allocation), Conservative Hybrid Funds (higher debt allocation), Balanced Advantage Funds (dynamic allocation between equity and debt).

- *Exchange-Traded Funds (ETFs):*
  Traded on stock exchanges like stocks. Offer real-time pricing and lower expense ratios.

- *Solution-Oriented Funds:*
  Designed for specific goals like retirement or children's education. Longer lock-in period.

Based on Asset Allocation:

- *Equity-Oriented Funds:*
  Invest in equity at least 65-80% and in debt 0-35%.

- *Debt-Oriented Funds:*
  Invest in debt at least 65-80% and in equity 0-35%.

- *Balanced/Hybrid Funds:*
  Invest in equity at least 40-60% and in debt 40-60%.

- *Money Market Funds:*
  Invest in short-term instruments like Treasury bills. This fund focused on capital preservation with moderate returns.

Allocation of Equity and Debt in one table:

Type of Fund	Equity Allocation	Debt Allocation	Risk Level	Suitable For
Large-Cap Equity Fund	80%-100%	0%-20%	High	Long-term capital growth.
Mid-Cap Equity Fund	80%-100%	0%-20%	High	Aggressive investors.
Debt Fund	0%-20%	80%-100%	Low to Moderate	Stable income.
Aggressive Hybrid Fund	65%-80%	20%-35%	Moderate to High	Balanced risk-reward.
Conservative Hybrid Fund	10%-25%	75%-90%	Low to Moderate	Income with low risk.
Balanced Advantage Fund	Dynamic (30%-70%)	Dynamic (30%-70%)	Moderate	Market condition adaptability.
Index Fund	90%-100%	0%-10%	Moderate to High	Passive investment.

Mutual funds are an excellent option for both beginners and experienced investors, offering flexibility and a range of choices to meet financial goals. Proper research and alignment with your risk profile can help you maximize returns.

***

Chapter 3

Assess Your Current Financial Situation:

Income: Calculate your total monthly income.

Expenses: Identify fixed and discretionary expenses.

Savings: Determine how much you can set aside for

investments after covering essential needs.

Emergency Fund: Ensure you have at least 3–6 months of living expenses saved in a liquid fund.

Define Your Financial Objectives

Financial goals into three categories,

- *Short-Term Goals (0–3 years):*
Invest for emergency fund and savings for a vacation, car, or wedding. Fund Type: **Liquid funds, ultra-short-term funds**, or **low-risk debt funds**.

- *Medium-Term Goals (3–7 years):*
Invest for children's education, purchase a home or renovation etc. Fund Type: **Balanced hybrid funds** or **debt funds** with moderate risk.

- *Long-Term Goals (7+ years):*
Invest for wealth creation, retirement corpus. Fund Type: **Equity funds, ELSS,** or **aggressive hybrid funds**.

Sample Investment Goal Plan:

Goal	Amount Needed	Time	Monthly SIP	Fund Type
Emergency Fund	2 Lakh	1 years	15000.00/-	Liquid Funds
Children's Education	6 Lakh	6 years	8000.00/-	Balanced Advantage Funds
Retirement Corpus	1 Cr	25 Years and above	6000.00/-	Equity Funds

By setting clear goals, calculating your required investments, and choosing the right mutual funds, you can create a customized investment plan. The key to achieving your goals lies in disciplined investing, regular monitoring, and staying committed to your financial objectives.

Chapter 4

Risk tolerance is the level of risk you are willing and able to accept when investing your money. In mutual fund investments, understanding your risk tolerance is crucial as it influences the type of funds you choose, your investment strategy, and your ability to stay invested during market fluctuations.

Types of Risk Tolerance

- *Aggressive Risk Tolerance:*
  Willing to accept significant market fluctuations for potentially higher returns. Suitable funds are Equity funds, mid-cap, small-cap, or sectoral funds.

- *Moderate Risk Tolerance:*
  Moderate risk for balanced growth and stability. Suitable funds are Hybrid

funds, large-cap equity funds, balanced advantage funds.

- ***Conservative Risk Tolerance:*** Conservative risk for capital preservation and accept lower returns. Suitable funds are debt funds, liquid funds, or money market funds.

Risk and Return Matrix:

Risk Level	Expected Returns	Fund Type
High Risk	12% - 20%	Mid-Cap, Small-Cap, Sectoral Funds
Moderate Risk	8% - 12%	Balanced Funds, Large-Cap Funds
Low Risk	4% - 7%	Debt Funds, Liquid Funds

Adapting Risk Tolerance Over Time

- *Life Stages:*
  Early Career: Higher risk for aggressive growth.
  Mid-Career: Balanced risk for stability and growth.
  Pre-Retirement: Lower risk to preserve capital.
- *Market Conditions:*
  During bullish markets, you may feel more confident taking risks.
  In bearish markets, you may prefer safer investments.
- *Changing Goals:*
  As goals approach, shift to funds with lower risk to protect your accumulated wealth.

According to **"Rule of 100"** is a simple guideline used to determine the ideal allocation of your investment portfolio between equity (stocks) and debt (bonds or other safer investments) based on your age and risk tolerance. It provides a starting point for asset allocation by factoring in your age and remaining investment horizon.

Formula:

- Percentage in Equity=100–Your Age
- Percentage in Debt=Your Age

Example Allocation Using the Rule of 100

Age	Debt Allocation (%)	Equity Allocation (%)
25	25	75
40	40	60
52	52	48
70	70	30

Conclusion

Understanding your risk tolerance ensures you select mutual funds that align with your comfort level and financial goals. Balancing risk with expected returns helps you stay invested through market cycles, minimizing stress and maximizing wealth creation over time. Regularly reassessing your risk tolerance and adjusting your portfolio accordingly is key to a successful investment journey.

***

Chapter 5

Evaluating the Performance of Mutual Funds

Effective performance evaluation involves assessing both quantitative metrics, such as returns and risk measures, and qualitative factors, such as fund management and strategy. By thoroughly analysing these aspects, investors can make informed decisions about whether to invest in, hold, or exit a particular mutual fund.

Quantitative Analysis

- *Return Analysis*
  - **Historical Returns**: Compare the fund's past performance over different time periods (1 year, 3 years, 5 years, etc.).

- **Absolute vs. Relative Performance**: Check whether the fund has outperformed its benchmark index or peer group.

- ➢ *Risk-Adjusted Returns*
  - **Sharpe Ratio**: Measures the fund's returns per unit of risk taken (higher is better).
  - **Treynor's Ratio**: Focuses on downside risk, giving a clearer picture of negative returns.
  - **Alpha**: Indicates the fund's ability to outperform its benchmark after adjusting for risk.
  - **Beta**: Reflects the fund's sensitivity to market movements (less than 1 indicates lower volatility than the market).

- ➢ *Volatility*
  - **Standard Deviation**: Measures the fund's price fluctuations.
  - **Max Drawdown**: The largest single drop from peak to trough over a specific period.

➢ *Fund Size and Liquidity*
  - AUM (Assets Under Management): a fund's too small may lack stability, while one that's too large could face efficiency issues.
  - Ensure the fund is sufficiently liquid for easy redemption.

➢ *Expense Ratio*
  - A lower expense ratio means more of your money stays invested, contributing to better long-term returns. Actively managed funds usually have higher expense ratios compared to passive funds like index funds or ETFs.

Qualitative Analysis

➢ *Fund Manager Performance and AMC*
  - Assess the fund manager's experience, tenure, and track record with the fund and other funds. Consistency in the fund's strategy under the current management.

- Choose a fund managed by a trusted and well-established AMC (Assets Management Company).

➢ *Portfolio Allocation*
- Sector allocation: avoids funds overly concentrated in a single sector.
- Diversification: look for funds with well-diversified portfolio across industries and asset classes.

➢ *Investment Strategy*
- Understand the fund's investment objective (e.g., growth, value, income).
- Ensure the strategy aligns with your investment goals and risk tolerance.

***

Chapter 6

Understanding Investment Styles in Mutual Funds:

Mutual funds follow specific investment styles to manage their portfolio and generate returns. The primary styles are **Growth** and **Value**. Understanding these styles is crucial for aligning a mutual fund with your financial goals, risk appetite, and investment strategy.

Growth Investment Style

Growth funds focus on investing in companies that exhibit higher-than-average growth rates, typically in terms of revenue, earnings, or market share. Invest in sectors like technology, healthcare, or emerging industries. Have higher price-to-earnings (P/E) or price-to-book (P/B) ratios.

Advantages:

Potential for significant capital appreciation.

Suitable for long-term investors willing to accept volatility.

Value Investment Style

Value funds invest in undervalued companies, which are priced lower than their intrinsic value based on fundamental analysis. Focus on companies with strong fundamentals but temporarily out-of-favour in the market. Lower P/E or P/B ratios compared to growth stocks.

Advantages:

Lower volatility compared to growth funds.

Potential for steady returns and downside protection.

Important Note:

> **P/E Ratio**: Indicates how expensive the stock is relative to its earnings. Higher values suggest higher expectations for future growth.
>
> **P/B Ratio**: Indicates how much investors are paying relative to the company's net asset value. Lower values may suggest the stock is undervalued.

***

Chapter 7

Passive vs. Active Mutual Funds

When investing in mutual funds, choosing between **active** and **passive funds** is an important decision. Both have unique characteristics, advantages, and drawbacks that can impact your investment strategy. Here's a detailed comparison to help you decide.

Active Mutual Funds

Active funds are managed by professional fund managers who actively select stocks, bonds, or other securities to outperform a benchmark index.

Characteristics:

- To outperform the market or a benchmark index.
- Managers can adjust the portfolio based on market conditions, trends, or insights.
- Requires constant monitoring and decision-making by fund managers.

Passive Mutual Funds

Passive funds aim to replicate the performance of a benchmark index, such as the Nifty 50 or S&P 500, by investing in the same securities in the same proportion.

Characteristics:

- Match (not beat) the benchmark index performance.
- Lower expense ratios mean more of the returns stay with the investor.

<u>**Key Differences Between Active and Passive Funds**</u>

Feature	Active fund	Passive fund
Management Style	Active (fund manager driven)	Passive (index replication)
Risk	Higher (managerial and market risk)	Lower (no managerial risk)
Returns	Can outperform or underperform	Matches benchmark returns
Expense Ratio	High (1-2%)	Low (0.1-0.5%)

Conclusion

- **Passive Funds**: Best for cost-conscious, low-risk investors who prefer predictable returns.
- **Active Funds**: Suitable for investors seeking potentially higher returns and willing to accept higher risks and costs.

***

Chapter 8

Reviews and Ratings for Mutual Funds

Reviews and ratings are valuable tools for assessing mutual funds, as they provide insights into a fund's performance, risk profile, and management quality.

Look for in Ratings

Mutual fund ratings typically summarize performance and risk factors into easily understood scores or stars.

- *Star Ratings*

5 Stars: Excellent past risk-adjusted returns. **3 Stars**: Average performance relative to peers. **1 Star**: Underperformed relative to peers.

- *CRISIL Ratings*

  Ratings are based on historical performance, consistency, and downside protection. Funds are ranked from **1 (best performing fund)** to **5 (worst performing fund)**.

- *Risk o metre*

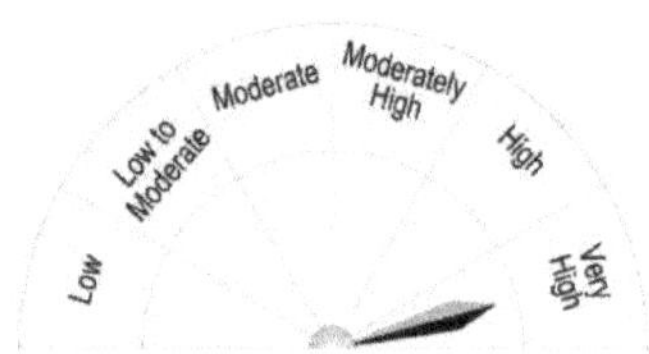

  The **Risk-o-Meter** is a valuable tool for investors to measure the risk level of a mutual fund, helping them make more informed decisions based on their personal risk appetite.

Understanding Reviews

  Mutual fund reviews often provide qualitative insights, including in fund manager's expertise, fund strategy, performance of fund and investor sentiment.

Conclusion:

Reading mutual fund reviews and ratings can help you:

- Understand a fund's strengths and weaknesses.
- Identify top-performing funds.
- Make informed decisions that align with your investment goals and risk tolerance.

***

Chapter 9

Check Exit Load and Tax Implications

When investing in mutual funds, understanding the **exit load** and **tax implications** is critical for evaluating the true cost and returns of your investment.

Exit Load

Exit load is a fee charged by the mutual fund house if you redeem your units within a specified time period after investment.

Exit Load=Redeemed Amount ×
Exit Load Percentage.

Usually, 1% if redeemed within 1 year on equity mutual fund, 0.25%-1%, depending on the holding period on debt mutual fund, no exit load on ELSS fund but there's a mandatory 3-year lock-in period.

Tax Implications

The tax treatment of mutual funds depends on the type of fund, holding period, and applicable tax laws in your country (India). Here all taxation is updated according to budgets on 23 July 2024.

Tax on Equity Funds		
Capital Gains	**Holding Period**	**Tax Rate**
Short-Term Capital Gains (STCG)	Less than 1 year or 12 months.	20% on capital gain.
Long-Term Capital Gains (LTCG)	More than 1 year or 12 months.	12.5% on gains exceeding ₹1.25 lakh.
Tax on Debt Funds		
Short-Term Capital Gains (STCG)	Less than 2 years.	Taxed as per the investor's income tax slab.

Long-Term Capital Gains (LTCG)	More than 2 years.	Tax slab rates no indexation benefit. (If investment before 1st April, 2023, 2years complete, then LTCG of 12.5%.)

Tax on Hybrid Funds

Based on the equity or debt proportion:

If **equity exposure > 65%**, taxed like equity funds.

If **equity exposure < 65%**, taxed like debt funds.

Tax-Saving Mutual Funds (ELSS)

- Equity Linked Savings Schemes (ELSS) offer tax benefits under **Section 80C**.
- Maximum deduction: ₹1.5 lakh per financial year.
- Lock-in period: 3 years.
- LTCG on ELSS is taxed at **12.5%** beyond ₹1.25 lakh.

Tax on Dividend Income

The tax rate is based on the individual's applicable income tax slab.

- Dividend Income Below ₹5,000, no tax.
- If total dividend exceeds ₹5,000 in a financial year, **TDS of 10%** is deducted by

> the company or mutual fund distributing the dividend. It is taxed based on the individual's **income tax slab**.

Conclusion:

- To minimize exit load and taxes, align your investment horizon with the fund's recommended holding period and redemption rules.
- Always plan withdrawals strategically.
- Consult a financial advisor your investments to your financial goals and tax situation.

***

Chapter 10

Mutual Fund Factsheet

A **mutual fund factsheet** is a detailed document published by an asset management company (AMC) to provide key information about a mutual fund. It serves as a concise summary of the fund's performance, objectives, portfolio composition, and other essential details, helping investors make informed decisions.

Steps to Download a Mutual Fund Factsheet

i.   Go to the official website of the Asset Management Company (AMC) managing the mutual fund. Example like HDFC Mutual Fund, ICICI Prudential Mutual Fund, etc.

ii. Look for sections like "Mutual Funds," "Resources," "Investors," or "Downloads." Or Some AMCs may have a direct "Factsheets" or "Fund Performance" tab.
iii. Choose the specific fund or category of funds you're interested in. The factsheets are usually organized by month, quarter, or specific fund categories (e.g., equity, debt, hybrid).
iv. Then download latest fund factsheet.

Key Details in a Mutual Fund Factsheet

A mutual fund factsheet provides an overview of the fund's performance, portfolio, and investment strategy. Here's what you'll typically find:

Fund Overview

- **Fund Name:** Name of the mutual fund.
- **Fund Category:** Type (e.g., equity, debt, hybrid).
- **Fund Manager(s):** Names and profiles of fund managers.
- **Launch Date:** Date the fund was introduced.

2. Net Asset Value (NAV)

- **Current NAV:** Per-unit price of the fund.
- **NAV History:** Recent NAV trends.

3. Investment Objective

- Describes the fund's goal (e.g., long-term capital growth, income generation).

4. Performance Data

- **Returns:** Annualized and absolute returns over different timeframes (1 year, 3 years, 5 years).
- **Benchmark Comparison:** Comparison against relevant indices (e.g., NIFTY, S&P 500).
- **Trailing and Rolling Returns:** Consistency of returns over periods.

5. Portfolio Composition

- **Asset Allocation:** Percentage split between equity, debt, cash, etc.
- **Sector Allocation:** Distribution of investments across industries or sectors.
- **Top Holdings:** List of major stocks or bonds in the portfolio.

6. Risk Metrics

- **Standard Deviation:** Volatility of fund returns.
- **Sharpe Ratio:** Risk-adjusted returns.

- **Beta:** Sensitivity to market movements.

7. Fees and Expenses

- **Expense Ratio:** Percentage of the fund's assets used for management and administration.
- **Exit Load:** Penalty for redeeming units within a specified time.

8. Fund Statistics

- **AUM (Assets Under Management):** Total value of assets managed by the fund.
- **Turnover Ratio:** Indicates portfolio turnover frequency.

9. Additional Information

- SIP (Systematic Investment Plan) details.
- Tax implications.

Important Note:

> **NAV (Net Asset Value)** in a mutual fund is the price of one unit of the fund. The **NAV changes daily** based on the fund's performance and market conditions.

In essence, a mutual fund factsheet is a valuable resource that condenses critical information into a single document, making it easier for investors to evaluate and choose mutual funds.

***

> **"Mutual Fund investments are subject to market risks, read all scheme related documents carefully."**

Chapter 11
(Investment Thumb Rule)

❖ <u>**Rule of 72**</u>

The **Rule of 72** is a simple way to estimate how long it will take for an investment to double in value, given a fixed annual rate of return. It is a quick, approximate calculation commonly used in personal finance and investing.

Formula:

Time to Double (in years)

$$\text{Time to Double (in years)} = \frac{72}{\text{Annual Rate of return}(\%)}$$

Example:

10% Annual Return:

$$\text{Time to Double (in years)} = \frac{72}{10} = 7.2 \text{ years.}$$

6% Annual Return:

$$\text{Time to Double (in years)} = \frac{72}{6} = 12 \text{ years.}$$

❖ <u>**Rule of 70**</u>

The **Rule of 70** is a simple way to estimate how long it will take for the value of money to halve due to inflation. It helps you understand the impact of inflation on your purchasing power and, consequently, your wealth.

$$\text{Time for Money to Halve (in years)} = \frac{70}{Inflation\ Rate(\%)}.$$

The result tells you how many years it will take for your wealth or purchasing power to lose **half** of its value.

Example:

Inflation Rate: 5% Time to Halve $= \frac{70}{5} =$ 14 years.

If inflation is 5% annually, ₹100 today will have the

purchasing power of ₹50 in about 14 years.

⁕

❖ <u>**50-30-20 Rule**</u>

The **50-30-20 Rule** is a simple budgeting guideline to help you manage your finances effectively by dividing your income into three main categories:

50% - Needs

Half of your income should be allocated to essential expenses or necessities, such as: rent, utilities, groceries, insurance premium, transportation etc.

30% - Wants

30% of your income can be spent on discretionary items or non-essentials that enhance your quality of life: Dining out, Entertainment (movies, subscriptions, etc.), Travel and vacations, shopping, hobbies etc.

20% - Savings

The remaining 20% should be used to build wealth, such as: Emergency fund savings, Investments (mutual funds, stocks, gold, etc.), Retirement savings (e.g., PPF, EPF, or pension funds).

❖ <u>10-5-3 Rule</u>

The **10-5-3 Rule** is a simple guideline used in investing to set realistic expectations for the average annual returns of different asset classes over the long term. It is not a hard rule but rather a general benchmark based on historical data.

10% - Equity (Stocks)

Historically, stocks (equity investments) tend to generate an average annual return of around **10%** over the long term.

- Assumes investing in a diversified stock portfolio or index funds.
- The actual return varies based on market conditions, but this is a typical average.

5% - Bonds

Bonds or fixed-income investments tend to generate an average annual return of around **5%**.

- This applies to high-quality bonds or government securities.
- Bonds provide stability and predictable returns but usually lower than stocks.

3% - Cash

Cash or cash-equivalent investments (e.g., savings accounts, fixed deposits, or money market funds) typically yield around **3%** annually.

- These are the safest options but are unlikely to outpace inflation in the long term.

Example:

If you invest ₹1,00,000 equally into stocks, bonds, and cash:

- **Stocks (10%)**: ₹33,333 grows to ~₹89,285 in 10 years.
- **Bonds (5%)**: ₹33,333 grows to ~₹54,246 in 10 years.
- **Cash (3%)**: ₹33,333 grows to ~₹44,769 in 10 years.

❖ <u>**8-4-3 Rule of Compounding**</u>

The **8-4-3 Rule of Compounding** is a guideline often used to illustrate the power of compounding interest and its long-term benefits.

1. **8**: If you save or invest consistently for **8 years**, you will accumulate a significant starting base of wealth due to your contributions.

2. **4**: By continuing the same pattern for **4 more years**, your investment will grow primarily due to the returns on your earlier investments (interest on interest).

3. **3**: If you stay invested for another **3 years**, the compounding effect amplifies significantly, and your returns start to outweigh your contributions.

Why It Matters:
- The rule emphasizes **time** as a crucial factor in wealth creation through compounding.

- Early investments grow much larger than later ones because of the snowball effect of interest or returns.

Example:

Suppose you invest ₹10,000 annually with a 10% annual return:

- After **8 years**, you will have contributed ₹80,000, which will have grown to approximately ₹114,000.
- After **4 more years** (12 years in total), your investment will have grown to roughly ₹210,000.
- After another **3 years** (15 years in total), your investment grows to about ₹345,000.

This rule serves as a practical illustration of how staying disciplined and allowing time to work in your favour can lead to exponential growth.

❖ <u>**100 minus age rules**</u>

The **100 minus age rule** is a widely used guideline in financial planning for asset allocation. It helps determine the proportion of investments in **equities** (stocks or stock mutual funds) versus **fixed-income instruments** (like bonds or other safer investments) based on an investor's age and risk tolerance.

Formula:

Percentage in Equities=100–Your Age
Percentage in Fixed-
Income Investments=Your Age

Explanation:

Younger investors: They have a longer investment horizon and can take on more risk. Hence, a higher percentage of their portfolio can be allocated to equities, which typically offer higher returns over the long term.
Example: A 25-year-old would allocate **75% to equities** (100 - 25) and **25% to fixed income.**

Older investors: As they approach retirement, they need to focus on capital preservation and stable returns. A greater proportion of their portfolio is allocated to fixed-income investments. *Example:* A 60-year-old would allocate **40% to equities** (100 - 60) and **60% to fixed income.**

⁘

❖ <u>4% withdrawal rule</u>

The **4% withdrawal rule** is a retirement planning guideline designed to help retirees determine how much they can safely withdraw from their retirement savings each year without running out of money.

The rule suggests:
- In the first year of retirement, withdraw **4% of your total retirement savings**.
- In subsequent years, adjust the withdrawal amount to account for **inflation** (to maintain purchasing power).

Example:

Suppose you have ₹1,000,000 saved for retirement.

In the first year, withdraw **₹40,000** (4% of ₹1,000,000).

If inflation is 2% the following year, withdraw **₹40,800** (to reflect a 2% increase).

Purpose:

The goal is to provide a consistent income stream while minimizing the risk of depleting retirement savings during your lifetime.

❖ <u>**Emergency fund rule**</u>

The **emergency fund rule** is a guideline to help individuals determine how much money to set aside in a readily accessible account to cover unexpected expenses or financial emergencies, such as medical bills, job loss, or major home repairs. It is equivalent to

3 to 6 months' worth of essential living expenses.

Who Needs 3 Months?
* Single-income households with stable jobs.
* People with multiple sources of income or lower financial obligations.

Who Needs 6 Months or More?
Single-income households with dependents.
Freelancers, gig workers, or those with irregular income.
People working in industries prone to layoffs.

Where to Keep the Emergency Fund?
Use liquid and safe financial instruments, such as: High-yield savings accounts, Fixed deposits (short-term), Money market accounts.

❖ <u>1-3-5-10 rule of investment horizon</u>

The **1-3-5-10 rule of investment horizon** is a simple framework that helps investors choose the right type of investment based on their time horizon and risk tolerance.

1-Year Horizon:

Capital preservation with minimal risk. Short-term goals, the focus is on liquidity and safety rather than growth.

Recommended Investments: Savings accounts or fixed deposits, Money market funds, Short-term debt funds.

3-Year Horizon:

With a slightly longer horizon, you can take limited risks while focusing on stable returns.

Recommended Investments: Short-term debt funds or corporate bond funds, Hybrid funds (a mix of debt and equity), Balanced advantage funds.

5-Year Horizon:

Over five years, equity markets typically provide better returns, and the risk of short-term volatility decreases.

Recommended Investments: Equity-oriented balanced funds, Large-cap equity funds, Index funds.

10-Year Horizon:

A longer horizon allows you to withstand market fluctuations and benefit from the power of compounding. *Recommended Investments:* Equity mutual funds (large-cap, mid-cap, or small-cap based on risk appetite), Index funds or exchange-traded funds (ETFs), Stocks (direct equity).

* * *

❖ <u>40% Retirement Rule</u>

The **40% Retirement Rule** is a financial planning guideline that suggests retirees should aim to replace at least **40% of their pre-retirement income from their retirement savings or investments**, with the remaining income typically coming from other sources like pensions or Social Security. This rule helps determine how much income your retirement savings should generate to sustain your lifestyle.

Total Income Requirement:

Retirees generally need **70-80% of their pre-retirement income** to maintain their lifestyle. The **40% rule** specifies that **40% of this income** should come from personal savings and investments.

Retirement Income:

40% from retirement savings or investments and **60% from guaranteed income sources** like social security, pensions or annuities.

Example:

Pre-Retirement Income: ₹100,000/year.

Retirement Income Need: ₹80,000/year, 80% of Pre-retirement income.

In this 80%, 40% from savings or investment account (₹32,000/year) and another 60% from other sources like social security, pensions or annuities (₹48,000/year).

❖ **<u>Debt-to-Income (DTI) Ratio Rule</u>**

The **Debt-to-Income (DTI) Ratio Rule** is a financial guideline that measures the percentage of your gross monthly income used to pay debts. It helps evaluate your financial health and determines whether you can comfortably manage additional debt, such as a loan or mortgage.

Formula:

$$\text{DTI Ratio} = \frac{Total\ Monthly\ Debt\ Payments}{Gross\ Monthly\ Income} \times 100.$$

<u>Recommended DTI</u>

43% and Above (High Risk):

Indicates a higher likelihood of financial stress. This is the maximum DTI allowed for **Qualified Mortgages** under U.S. guidelines.

37% to 43% (Acceptable):

Borrowers in this range might be more financially stretched. Some lenders may approve loans, especially if other factors (e.g., credit score or savings) are strong.

36% or Lower (Ideal):

Indicates strong financial health and the ability to manage debts comfortably.

Most lenders consider a DTI of **36% or below** as safe.

Example:

Let assume a person's gross monthly income is ₹50,000 and monthly debt payments are: mortgage = ₹12,000/-; car = ₹3,000/-; credit card bill = ₹2,000/-.

Total debt payment is ₹17,000/- in a month.

$$\therefore \text{DTI Ratio} = \frac{17000}{50000} \times 100 = 34.$$

The DTI is 34%, which is within the ideal range.

❖ <u>10% Savings Rule</u>

The **10% Savings Rule** is a simple and widely recommended financial guideline that encourages individuals to save at least **10% of their income** for future needs, such as building an emergency fund, retirement, or other financial goals.

If your monthly income is 50,000/- then 10%=5,000/- is savings must.

Purpose of the 10% Rule:

- Create a financial safety (emergency fund).
- Build long-term wealth through investments.
- Save for major financial goals like buying a home, children's education, or vacations.

Benefits of the 10% Rule:
- Encourages financial discipline on savings.
- It is easy to simple and achievable your financial goals.

www.ingramcontent.com/pod-product-compliance
Lightning Source LLC
Chambersburg PA
CBHW041920130726
48007CB00014B/142